Link-up

G000164962

A pronunciati

Colin Mortimer

Drawings by Daria Gan

Cambridge University Press

Cambridge
London · New York · Melbourne

For Edward

Published by the Syndics of the Cambridge University Press
The Pitt Building, Trumpington Street, Cambridge CB2 1RP
Bentley House, 200 Euston Road, London NW1 2DB
32 East 57th Street, New York, NY 10022, USA
296 Beaconsfield Parade, Middle Park, Melbourne 3206, Australia

© Cambridge University Press 1977

ISBN 0 521 21353 3

First published 1977

Printed in Great Britain at the
University Press, Cambridge

Introduction

Link-up consists of 50 dialogues designed to encourage upper intermediate and more advanced students to link words together smoothly and naturally, in connected speech, in the way that native speakers normally do. It aims to help especially those learners who tend to pronounce each word as though it were isolated, or to make excessive use of the glottal stop before words beginning with vowels.

Intensive, contextualised practice is provided in linking:

1. Words ending in a *consonant* sound to words beginning with a *vowel* sound:

     e.g.   read‿it   brush‿up   sing‿it

2. Words ending in a *vowel* sound to words beginning with a *vowel* sound:

     e.g.   you‿are   I‿ought   after‿all

Each dialogue features a particular link or combination of links, the basis of organisation and selection being place and manner of articulation. So, for example, Dialogues 1 and 2 are devoted to linking p and b to words beginning with a vowel; Dialogue 26 focusses on t, d, n and l, which have first been practised individually in separate dialogues.

Using the book

There are many ways of using the dialogues and variety is important. But in general it is suggested that before students practise the dialogues they should hear them spoken by a good model or models, to get a sense of the meaning and pronunciation of the whole. After this they can work from judicious and varied practice of individual phrases and lines to a fluent performance of the full dialogue in chorus, groups and pairs. Dialogues should be constantly revised, and some may usefully be memorised.

Linking final consonant sounds to initial vowel sounds

One practice technique which many students find helpful is to

3

treat the final consonant sound of a word as though it were
transferred to the next word:

    e.g. Practise   put it off
          as though it were   pu-ti-toff

Used with care, this device helps to promote good linking. It
should be noted, however, that though *linked* to words beginning
with vowel sounds, final consonant sounds are not usually in fact
fully *transferred* in English. Thus, for example, in the phrase
'stop anywhere', the p at the end of 'stop' is not strongly aspirated
as it would be if 'any' became 'penny'. Though linked, 'stop' and
'anywhere' retain their identity.

Linking 'r'

When a word ending with a letter 'r' precedes a word beginning
with a vowel sound, the 'r' is usually pronounced, and this linkage
is indicated in the text:

    e.g.   after all

Linking final vowel sounds to initial vowel sounds

To help students to link vowel sounds to vowel sounds, a small w
or j is included with the linker:

    e.g. do it   he ate some
       w   j

Here again, used judiciously, this device will help to promote
natural linking. Care should be taken, however, not to exaggerate
the link to a full, strong w or j, resulting in

    do-wit   he-yet

Comprehension and summary

A recognised difficulty in teaching pronunciation is how to
maintain improvements when the emphasis shifts from conscious
pronunciation practice to concentration on *meaning*. One way of
mitigating this difficulty is to use as a basis for simple oral comprehension or summary language that has recently been practised
for pronunciation. Such work forms a useful interim stage in that
it diverts some attention to meaning without distracting too much
attention from pronunciation:

Comprehension (Dialogue 20):
      Question What did B win?
      Answer   An apple.
      Question What did A win?
      Answer   An orange.
      Question What did John win?
      Answer   An air ticket.
Summary (Dialogue 3)
      The man liked to read in bed, but his wife wanted him to put
      the light off. He didn't want to put it off... etc.

The recording

All of the dialogues are recorded on cassette, and all except the
last three are preceded by a *listen and repeat section*, with gaps on
the tape for student repetition. In this preliminary section, short,
key items from the forthcoming dialogue are drilled intensively.

  e.g. A. Win anything?
           Did you win anything?
           Did you win anything?
       B. An apple
          An apple
          I won an apple
          I won an apple
       A. An orange
          I won an orange
          I won an orange
The dialogues themselves are, of course, recorded without gaps,
but teachers with a class, or students working individually, can use
the pause and rewind mechanisms of their machines to play and
repeat sections on which they may wish to concentrate.

Paced reading

Students often find it helpful to read *along with* the tape; to do this
kind of paced reading it may be advisable to turn down the volume
of the tape a little.

Note. Words printed in *italics* should be given extra emphasis.

Contents

1 p b

A   Don't tap its cage. Don't disturb it.

B   I hope it won't sleep all day.

A   It *needs* to sleep all day.

B   Why keep a pet that can do nothing but sleep all day?

A   Stop it!

B   Pop out! Pop out, Sammy! A drop of water, Sammy?

A   Oh, Bob, I hope it *bites* you!

B   Hm! It's gone back to sleep in my *hand*!

A   Well, don't disturb it.

2 p b

A   Now, the psychological test. Ready? Quickly say the first verb each
    noun brings to your mind. Don't stop and think. Is that clear? Don't
    stop and think.

B   I hope it's clear, yes.

A   Right. The first noun . . . 'Handbag.'

B   Grab. Grab a handbag.

A   'Bank.'

B   Rob a bank.

A   'Man.'

B   Stab a man.

A   Stab a man. Mm . . . er . . .

B   Don't stop and think, Doctor! Don't stop and think!

3 t d

A   Put it off. Turn the light off.

B   I need it on. I've got a lot of reading to do.

A   Read it downstairs. I can't sleep with the light on.

B   Get under the bedclothes.

A   *You* get under the bedclothes.

B   Have you got a torch?

8

4 t d

A I'm called 'Pat', and I don't like my name.

B It isn't attractive.

A But 'Pat' isn't as bad as some names. What about 'Dot'?

B Dot isn't attractive.

A Oh, no. Dot isn't at *all* nice, no . . . Even
   Pat isn't as bad as *Dot* . . . What are *you* called, by the way?

B You've guessed it!

5 k g

A I'd like a walk – I think I'll take the dog out, Betty.

B I'd like a drink – I think I'll go to the 'Duke of York' and drink a
   cool lager.

A *You'd* like a drink, Betty? *You'd* like a drink? Oh, well . . .
   Let's *both* take the dog out, then!

B Fine.

A No, dammit. Let's leave the dog at *home*!

6   k g

A   I learnt this card trick on holiday. Now . . . pick a card.

B   Pick any card.

A   I can take *any* card?

B   Take any card you like.

A   I think I'll take . . . *this* card.

B   Take any card but that.

7   tʃ dʒ

A   My watch is ready. Will you fetch it for me?

B   Yes. Will they charge anything, d'you think?

A   They *shouldn't* charge anything. The watch is new.

B   Oh . . . but there's *one* charge I mustn't forget . . .

A   Darling, no! My lipstick! You'll smudge it!

B   Mm! Nice!

A   Pay the delivery charge *after*, darling!

8   tʃ dʒ

A   George, it's not possible! Your *leg*! You *can't* judge a beauty contest today.

B   You know where my crutch is, Bertha.

A   Of course, dear. But George, I really think you should . . .

B   Fetch it!

9 f v

A   I give all my parties from five until seven . . .
       Arrive at five exactly, please.

B   Arrive at five – of course, Sir.

A   Leave at seven, punctually.

B   Leave at seven, Sir. Yes, Sir.

A   Then move off and have a really good time. Right?

B   Sir?

A   Well, my parties *do* have a . . . reputation, don't they?
       Mm?

10 f v

A   Give it to me!

B   I can't give it. I don't *have* it.

A   I *know* you have it! There! The safe, over there!

B   *If* I have it, . . . I have it . . .

A   Give it to me *now*!

B   . . . I have it . . . HERE!

A   AAAAAAARRRGGGGGGGH!!!!!

B   You see, Clive, enough is . . .

A   Aaaarggh!

B   . . . enough, old friend.

11 θ ð

A Are you going to the party with Alan?

B I can't go with Alan.

A Or with Eric?

B I can't go with Eric.

A Oh.

B Why don't *you* go with *both* of them?

A To tell you the truth, I can't go with *either*.

B You're not going?

A I'm going with Alec.

B With Alec? Both of us?

12 θ ð

A Breathe in.

B Hh.

A Breathe out.

B Hh.

A Breathe in, then breathe out, rapidly.

B Hh Hh. Hh Hh. Hh Hh.

A Well, Mrs Smith, I've told you month after month your health is first class now. No need to come next month, I think.

B It's worth it, Doctor. It's worth every penny.

A Oh, by the way, next month it'll be Dr Booth, I must tell you.

B Dr Booth – I don't know Dr Booth – is he nice?

A She's *very* nice.

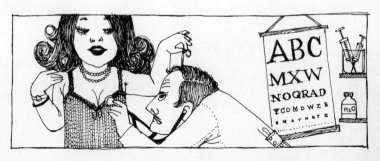

13 s z

A Is Alice in?

B Alice is out.

A Alice is always out.

B Alice is always out because Alice always gets invited.

A Well, *Pamela*'s in.

B As always.

A So put your best dress on, Pamela. Choose any place in town.

B The dance Alice is at.

A That's a good suggestion.

B Is it?

14 s z

A Is the boss in?

B The boss is *out*.

A The boss is *always* out.

B He's expected soon. He's at lunch.

A It's almost *four*!

B He's always in time for tea.

15 ∫

A   Don't push it. These things smash easily.

B   *I* shan't smash it.

A   Don't *push* it! You'll *smash* it!

B   Now . . . just one more little push, and then . . .
    Gosh, I'm terribly sorry.

A   I *told* you not to push it! I *told* you you'd . . .

B   Use that brush over there, will you?

A   I wish I'd never . . .

B   Good girl. Brush up the pieces nicely.

A   OH!

B   Good girl.

16 ∫

A   Your whisky, Sir. With the usual splash of soda.

B   Thank you. Now which dish is good today?

A   The fish is good.

B   Fresh, I hope?

A   Fresh, of course, Sir.

B   And to finish off . . .

A   The usual, Sir?

B   But with lemon squash, I think. Not soda.

14

17 m

A   Come into *this* room – it's warm in here.

B   Thank you.

A   You've come about Jim, I suppose.

B   Jim isn't doing well.

A   I'm afraid that's true.

B   Jim oughtn't to be bottom of the class.

A   But next term I think we'll see him improving.   I'm optimistic.

B   Last time I came I remember you said . . .

A   'I'm optimistic', yes. But this time I'm *especially* so. Now . . .
Tea? Jam? Plum or strawberry?

18 m

A   Come in.

B   I can't come in . . . I must go home in two minutes.

A   Come in for two minutes.

B   I wouldn't get home – I know *you*.

A   *I'll* come *out*, then.

B   Yes. Come along home if you like.

A   Mm!

B   Come and have supper.

A   Mm!!

B   Come and meet my mum and dad.

A   Mm . . .

19 n

A A loan of fifteen or sixteen thousand, Mr Brown.

B Well, *ten*, if fifteen or sixteen isn't possible.

A In a case like yours, Mr Brown, even a loan of one or two . . .

B Thousand?

A One or two . . .

B Hundred?

A One or two . . .

B Pounds?

A Would be more than I can arrange.

B Oh.

A I can offer you one . . .

B Gin and tonic?

A *Suggestion*, if you like.

20 n

A Did you win anything?

B I won an apple. Did *you* win anything?

A I won an orange.

B John won an air ticket.

A An air ticket to where?

B To London, I think. But he doesn't think he can afford the time to go. He hopes he can exchange the prize for something different.

A An orange, perhaps?

21 ŋ

A Sing a song, Elizabeth. Sing a nursery rhyme.
Please sing 'Sing a Song of Sixpence'. Sing it nicely for daddy.

B I'll sing it for sixpence.

22 ŋ

A Bring a ring and that lovely string of pearls.

B Any particular ring, Edwina?

A Bring a diamond ring, Alfred. Something a bit special.

B Yes. They'll be putting *everything* in the window today.

A Are you taking anything along, Alfred?

B Something appropriate, my love.

A Nothing *obtrusive*, Alfred?

B I'm taking a brick, dear.

23 l

A Avril isn't well, in fact.

B Ill again?

A I'll obviously have to cancel all engagements. Cancel our holiday. Cancel everything.

B Don't cancel anything till *I've* seen her.

A Dr Gale examined her. It's his considered medical opinion that . . .

B Avril *is* your wife now. But she's my girl and . . .

A You know her very well, of course, but . . .

B Tell Avril I'll come. Say you won't cancel *anything*.

A Well, I won't go to Paris by myself, certainly.

B I don't think you *will*, Anthony.

A   Next we'll interview Miss Val Underhill, I think.

B   Underhill? . . . Val Underhill? Erm . . . Did she fill in the form?

A   She did fill in the form.

B   Mm. Well it seems we didn't file it, then.

A   Well, if we've lost the form we'll obviously have to . . .

B   Sh!

A   Ah, good morning. Miss Underhill, I presume?

     Now, naturally we have your full application here . . .

B   All appropriate personal and professional information . . .

A   Nevertheless, we'd be grateful if you'd tell us . . .

B   It would be *useful* if you'd tell us something . . .

A   All about yourself, please.

25 p b m

A Rob, I'm up in the bedroom. Grab a drink. I'm almost ready.

B Plenty of time, actually. Shall we stop and see Tom on the way?

A Is Tom up again from town?

B Yes. Let's stop and see him a minute.

A Now! D'you like my new dress, darling?

B Ravishing!

A If we stop and see Tom, I'm afraid we'll be . . .

B Tom *is* my friend . . .

A Yes, darling, but . . .

B But you're not going to see him in *that* dress!
   I know Tom!

A Darling, how sweet!

26 t d n l

A What in the hell is *that*, Enid Evans?

B I bought it in a sale, Eddie.

A Well, it isn't *ideal*, to say the least, Enid.

B It isn't ideal, Eddie, no.

A In fact, I'd incline to call it . . .

B Well *don't* Eddie. Not unless you want your meal elsewhere.

A Sorry.

B Thank you.

A Enid, in fact now that I've looked at it *again*, I . . .

B Isn't it *awful*, Eddie?

27 t d n l s z

A   Can I ride it, please, uncle?

B   Yes, of course, if you ride it carefully.

A   Can I go fast on it?

B   Yes, if you go carefully.

A   I can't ride it outside, I suppose, uncle?

B   Perhaps it might be best if you practised in the garden a bit first.

A   Then can I ride it in the road?

B   Well, I'll see. Perhaps your dad wouldn't agree.

A   But I know dad *would* agree. Definitely.

B   Well, I'll ask.

A   Don't ask.

28 tʃ dʒ ʃ

A   Hush, Ida! Switch off the light! Look!

B   Don't be foolish, Agatha!

A   Didn't you see him dodge into the bush, Ida?

B   Dodge into the bush, indeed!...Oh!...Oh!!

A   Look! See him?

B   I wish Albert were here!

A   Courage, Ida! Come with me!

B   Oh dear!

A   Switch on the garden light! NOW!

B   Oh dear!

A   Albert!!

B   Albert!!

A   Albert, kindly leave that *bush* and come *here*!

29 tʃ dʒ ʃ s z

A   When will you finish it?

B   Finish it? Finish it? It's finished!

A   Wallace, as I always admit . . .

B   Yes?

A   I'm no judge of sculpture.

B   No.

A   No judge of such artistic . . .

B   No. You're no judge, Anna.

A   But Wallace, I wonder . . .

B   Yes?

A   Which is the *front*, Wallace?

B   Hah!

30   pb td kg mnŋ l

A   I hope if Mr Bebb isn't able to hold a quick, informal meeting today, Miss Rigg, I shall manage to come over there myself to talk to the men about this thing and settle it.
Have you got all that? Miss Rigg?

B   Miss Rigg isn't in, I'm afraid. Who's speaking, please?

31   fv θð

A   If Eve is with us . . .

B   Or Beth is with us . . .

A   We'll have a very good time.

B   If both Eve *and* Beth are with us . . .

A   Wow!

B   It'll *really* be worth it!

32   fv θð sz ʃ tʃ dʒ

A   If I pay five each to both of you . . .

B   Five each?

A   Six if I can.

B   Six isn't much, is it?

A   I might manage a bit more.

B   But this is a '*hush hush*' assignment!

A   Ssshhh!

33   pb td kg tʃ dʒ fv θð sz ʃ mnŋ l

A   One cup only, Mrs Lobb, I think . . . I diet, actually.
No bread, of course . . . Oh, that beautiful cake, if you like.
Not very big, I beg you . . . Oh, *too* much, I assure you. Well,
that's not *too* large, I suppose . . . If I *have* to have a double portion
please make the second slice small. Cream? On both – oh dear!
With even *more* cream? Really, this is excessive . . . I wish I
could persuade you not to . . .

B   Some jam on it?

A   Nothing else.

B   Ah.

A   The jam will indeed be the *climax*!

A   Don't stop, Iris. Rub it again.

B   I'm tired of rubbing your back, Arthur.

A   Iris Sprigg, I want you to know how much it *means* to me . . .
     I can't *manage* if I don't have it rubbed . . .

B   Put your teeth in.

A   I can't talk with all that plastic there.

B   Your face is *awful*. Push 'em in Arthur.

A   No. I can *sing* a lot better without those dental appliances.
     Listen!

35   r

A   After all, you're only twenty-four, Ann.

B   Mother, at twenty-four a girl's rather old.

A   At *fifty*-four a girl's rather *older*, isn't she?

B   But mother, I don't suppose father even *notices*.

A   Father appreciates your mother 'as nature intended'!

B   You're always nice. Where are you going, by the way?

A   To my regular appointment with the hairdresser, if you want to
     know.

B   For a shampoo?

A   I have some grey hair, at the roots – which nature *never* intended!

A   Pour the beer in here, in the kitchen, Peter.

B   Pour it here, Eric? Rather a queer place to pour beer.

A   Don't pour it *there*, idiot.

B   You said pour it here, Eric.

A   Here! Here in the glass! Not there on the floor!

B   Oh.

A   Peter isn't *clever*, is he?

B   I corroborate your unpalatable though veracious diagnosis.

A   What?

B   I corroborate your unpalatable though veracious diagnosis.

A   You think you're clever, I suppose?
      Here – clear up the mess.

     * *Note:* this dialogue introduces practice in detecting 'silent' as well as 'linking' r.

37

A   Do I have to do every question?

B   You ought to try.

A   How much time do I have?

B   We give you about two hours.

A   Two hours?

B   Those who are quick can go early.

A   And those who can't do it?

B   *They* can go early *too*, I suppose.

A   Good.

38

A   Who saw it?

B   *I* saw it.

A   You saw it where?

B   I saw it there. There.

A   Who else saw it?

B   Who else?

A   You understand that we have to ask these questions.

B   I don't know if...

A   Only *you* saw it?

B   Probably.

A   Do you often see... *things*?

B   It would be foolish to underestimate their powers...

A   We merely wish to ensure that... what's wrong?

B   Perhaps you ought to look... behind you.

39

A My thigh and my arm still hurt. I expect to be up tomorrow, though.

Tea or coffee or something? The coffee isn't very good.

B Thanks. Tea, I think.

A. Room Service? Could we have tea in Room Twenty, please? For two, please.

B I *am* sorry about the accident. We all miss you.

A Hm. I ought to learn to ski a bit better.

B Merely to *see* a bit better, Dick.

A I don't like to ski in glasses.

B If you can't see a *tree*, I think you should wear them.

40

A My fee isn't high, of course.

B How high *is* your fee, actually?

A I always charge the lowest possible fee, I assure you.

B May I ask how much?

A I ask one hundred.

B A hundred?

A I invariably accept one hundred.

B I invariably offer *fifty*.

A I occasionally accept seventy-five.

B I occasionally pay it.

A Seventy-five?

B We agree?

A Reluctantly, of course.

B Of course.

41 ⌣w r ⌣j

A You say I can go out? Go anywhere?

B Yes. Go anywhere.

A Anywhere I like?

B Anywhere, of course. Though I ought to say we *are* expected to be back by five.

A *We* are?

B We *are*.

A *We*?

B I *am* required to *accompany* you, you understand.

42 ⌣w r. ⌣j

A That tree ought to *go*. We can't *see* anything for it.

B Surely you don't want to destroy our ancient tree?

A We can't *see* in here, and yet the sun's shining.

B Anyway, I adore it.

A I only say it spoils the view.

B And that tree always reminds me of mother.

A It's the *tree* I'm discussing. Don't bring your *mother* into it!

43

   ˇ   r   ˇ
   w   j

A   Go and see if Fay and Roy are able to come.

B   I'll go and *see*, of course.

A   They always say they *are* coming.

B   Then they always stay away.

A   Even so, I *like* Fay and Roy.

B   Oh, *I* like Fay and Roy.

A   But you're absolutely right.

B   I *am*?

A   Yes. Why *should* we invite them?

B   Well, we always *do*.

A   Oh, all right, then.

44

   ˇ   r   ˇ
   w   j

A   I expect you know Ian Green.

B   No, I don't know Ian Green.

A   Oh, I thought you *would*.

B   No, I don't.

A   I rather expected you *would*.

B   Why, I wonder? Is he influential?

A   His father is. Very influential: Magnus Green.

B   I know the *father*, of course.

A   I advise you to get to know the *son*.

B   Why all the hurry?

A   Mummy always knows best, dear.

45 ⌣ r ⌣ pb td kg tʃ dʒ
   w   j

A You're already a bit late. Where are you, anyway?

B Up at the club.

A Up at the club all this time?

B They had a match, actually. No point in rushing back, is there?
I'll get a snack in the bar and stay on here with the boys for a bit.
Celebrate our victory.

A That *Vickie* isn't in the bar, is she?

B Vickie? Who's Vickie? There's no one here except the boys.
Oh, I see! *Behind* the bar! Mm, she *is* rather dishy, isn't she?

A Dishy, indeed! Be your age, Edwin!

B I *am* my age, darling.

A Watch it! Or I'll be over there in *no* time! Bye dear.

B Bye love . . . Anyway, what about you and that new *milkman*?

46 ⌣ r ⌣ m n ŋ l
   w   j

A I'm on a long overdue holiday, that's where I am.

B When are you coming back?

A I don't know when I'm coming, actually.

B Where are you staying, anyway?

A I'm staying in a very interesting place.

B *Interesting* Olive?

A Boring as hell, actually. I'll be home in the morning, Edwin.

A   I wish I knew if you *are* or *aren't* coming with us.

B   I wish I knew myself if I am.

A   Surely the business isn't going to collapse if one of you goes out for a day, is it?

B   Of *course* it's not. But not *both* of us. If *I* go *out*, then *Willy* must stay *in*.

A   Why all the fuss about Willy? Willy's always out.

B   Willy's out *now*, actually. So it all depends on whether or not he returns, I'm sorry to say. I don't need to say any more, I suppose? Where are you off to?

A   I know where Willy is, I imagine. Though he may not know it, he's about to return in five minutes or less, is Willy. So be ready in five minutes.

B   Yes, Ada.

48   Revision

A   This dialogue appears again in almost identical form on the next page. But on the next page I've taken out all the links. What *you* are supposed to do is to practise a time or two from *this* page, and then turn over and do it without any help at all. Like to have a try at it?

B   I ought to have a try, I suppose.

31

49 Revision

A   This dialogue appears again in almost identical form on the previous page. But on *this* page I've taken out all the links. What *you* are supposed to do is to practise a time or two from *that* page, and then turn over and do it without any help at all. Like to have a try at it?

B   I've tried.

A   How did you do?

50 Conclusion

A   Well, anyway, I hope you'll continue to work on this very important aspect of the pronunciation of English, and that you've enjoyed the book. See you again, I hope.

B   (*Say anything you like here as long as you LINK IT UP appropriately!*)